THE 2012 MOON ALMANAC
(AND THE 2012 MOON CALENDAR CARD)

Copyright © Kim Long, 2011

The Experiment, LLC
260 Fifth Avenue
New York, NY 10001–6408
www.theexperimentpublishing.com

The Experiment's books are available at special discounts when purchased in bulk for premiums and sales promotions as well as for fundraising or educational use. For details, contact us at info@theexperimentpublishing.com.

Library of Congress Control Number: 2011934009

ISBN 978-1-61519-041-6
Ebook ISBN 978-1-61519-143-7

Cover design by Alison Forner
Cover photographs by iStock

Manufactured in Mexico
Distributed by Workman Publishing Company, Inc.
Distributed simultaneously in Canada by Thomas Allen & Son Limited
First published October 2011
10 9 8 7 6 5 4 3 2

THE EXPERIMENT BECAUSE EVERY BOOK IS A TEST OF NEW IDEAS

• THE 2012 MOON ALMANAC •

Contents

W9-BPJ-465

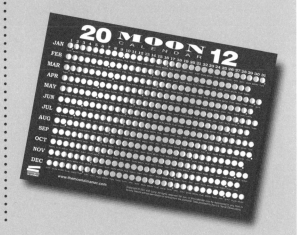

Welcome!

Almanacs have been around for thousands of years. The concept originated as a source of information about cycles of time, especially the movements of the Sun and Moon. The Moon itself predates the Sun as the predominate celestial timekeeper. It was a key visible element to mark the start of months, years, and religious holidays, but it was tough to coordinate with the solar year.

In modern times, the traditional concept of almanacs has expanded to include entertainment content, trivia, and general knowledge. Meanwhile, both printed and online sources provide ready access to detailed, accurate information about the Sun and the Moon. The Moon itself has been the object of signficant scientific study, with more underway. Astronauts landed on its surface in 1969, eliminating many unknowns, but it still remains an object of mystery and superstition to many.

With this publication, we return to the origins of the almanac genre, providing a new kind of annual reference, a source of useful, reliable, and informative facts about the Moon and its regular cycles. This almanac has its origins in *The Moon Calendar*, an annual publication that was born in 1981 and continues today in a unique new format—a pullout card attached to the back cover.

Our modern culture may no longer rely on the Moon as a guide to calendar cycles, but the remnants of past wonder continue. With nothing but the unaided eye, any adult or child can share in this age-old magic, continuing our unending fascination with our nearest celestial neighbor.

—Kim Long

TIME CONVERSIONS

PST Pacific Standard Time	MST Mountain Standard Time	CST Central Standard Time	EST Eastern Standard Time	UT Universal Standard Time
−8 hours	−7 hours	−6 hours	−5 hours	

DURING DAYLIGHT SAVING TIME, SUBTRACT 1 ADDITIONAL HOUR

DAYLIGHT SAVING TIME BEGINS March 11
DAYLIGHT SAVING TIME ENDS November 4

"Oh, swear not by the moon, the inconstant moon,
That monthly changes in her circled orb."
— WILLIAM SHAKESPEARE
(*Romeo and Juliet*, c. 1596)

Data used in *The 2012 Moon Almanac* and *The 2012 Moon Calendar Card* was provided by the U.S. Naval Observatory and other sources of astronomical information. The contents were produced with the guidance of Larry Sessions, astronomer.

2

• MOON DISTANCE •

The Moon orbits around the Earth on an elliptical path, an oval that puts it closer to us at some points in the lunar month. The closest point of this ellipse is the perigee; the point when it is farthest is the apogee.

The distance between these two extremes is about 10 percent, enough to create a visible difference in the size of the full moon—as much as 14 degrees, wider if it falls at one extreme or the other. This effect is compounded when the full moon is rising or setting; the closeness to the horizon and the proximity to trees, buildings, and other objects combine to produce this illusion.

On May 5 (May 6 for time zones east of the United States), the Moon will be at its closest to the Earth for the year and the closest in about nineteen years. Also on this day, the full moon will occur at almost the same point in time—within two minutes of the perigee—a rare co-incidence (informally called a "supermoon") that means the rising full moon will appear to be even larger than normal and could affect the height of tides.

The charts below are based on Universal Time (UT). See page 2 to correct for local time zones.

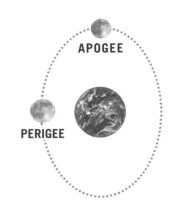

• MOON ORBIT STANDARDS •

AVERAGE DISTANCE	238,712 mi (384,400 km)
FARTHEST APOGEE	252,586 mi (406,740 km)
SHORTEST PERIGEE	221,331 mi (356,410 km)
AVERAGE DISTANCE IN EARTH DIAMETERS	30
ANOMALISTIC MONTH (Apogee to Apogee or Perigee to Perigee)	27 days 13 hrs 18 min 33.2 sec

PERIGEE			APOGEE		
January 17	21:29	229,327 mi (369,882 km)	January 2	20:20	250,839 mi (404,579 km)
February 11	18:33	228,110 mi (367,919 km)	January 30	17:43	242,594 mi (404,324 km)
March 10	10:03	224,687 mi (362,399 km)	February 27	14:03	251,014 mi (404,862 km)
April 7	17:00	214,988 mi (358,313 km)	March 26	6:05	251,583 mi (405,779 km)
• May 6	3:34	221,311 mi (356,953 km)	April 22	13:50	251,980 mi (406,420 km)
June 3	13:21	222,259 mi (358,482 km)	• May 19	16:14	251,999 mi (406,450 km)
July 1	18:02	224,658 mi (362,351 km)	June 16	1:25	243,474 mi (405,790 km)
July 29	8:31	220,390 mi (367,317 km)	July 13	16:48	250,965 mi (404,782 km)
August 23	19:40	229,233 mi (369,730 km)	August 10	10:53	242,474 mi (404,124 km)
September 19	2:53	226,764 mi (365,748 km)	September 7	6:01	250,663 mi (404,295 km)
October 17	1:03	223,617 mi (360,672 km)	October 5	0:44	251,200 mi (405,161 km)
November 14	10:23	221,563 mi (357,360 km)	November 1	15:31	251,750 mi (406,049 km)
December 12	23:15	221,385 mi (357,073 km)	November 28	19:36	251,946 mi (406,364 km)
			December 25	21:21	251,781 mi (406,099 km)

• CLOSEST OF THE YEAR   • FARTHEST OF THE YEAR

• 2012 •
MOON PHASES

	NEW MOON	FIRST QUARTER	FULL MOON	LAST QUARTER

• FULL MOON HISTORY •

JANUARY 21, 1799 English physician Edward Jenner introduced his ground-breaking vaccination for smallpox.

JANUARY 9, 1811 The first golf tournament for women was held at Musselburgh, Scotland.

SPRING EQUINOX	
March 20	5:14 AM UT
	12:14 AM EST
March 19	11:14 PM CST
	10:14 PM MST
	9:14 PM PST

JANUARY

FIRST QUARTER
1 6:15 AM UT
1:15 AM EST
12:15 AM CST
12/31 11:15 PM MST
10:15 PM PST

FULL MOON
9 7:30 AM UT
2:30 AM EST
1:30 AM CST
12:30 AM MST
8 11:30 PM PST
WOLF MOON

LAST QUARTER
16 9:08 AM UT
3:08 AM EST
2:08 AM CST
1:08 AM MST
12:08 AM PST

FEBRUARY

NEW MOON
23 7:39 AM UT
2:39 AM EST
1:39 AM CST
12:39 AM MST
1:39 PM PST

FIRST QUARTER
31 4:10 AM UT
30 11:10 PM EST
10:10 PM CST
9:10 PM MST
8:10 PM PST

FULL MOON
7 9:54 PM UT
4:54 PM EST
3:54 PM CST
2:54 PM MST
1:54 PM PST
SNOW MOON

LAST QUARTER
14 5:04 PM UT
1:04 PM EST
12:04 PM CST
11:04 AM MST
10:04 AM PST

MARCH

NEW MOON
21 10:35 PM UT
5:35 PM EST
4:35 PM CST
3:35 PM MST
2:35 PM PST

FIRST QUARTER
3/1 1:21 AM UT
29 8:21 PM EST
7:21 PM CST
6:21 PM MST
5:21 PM PST

FULL MOON
8 9:39 AM UT
4:39 AM EST
3:39 AM CST
2:39 AM MST
1:39 AM PST
WORM MOON

LAST QUARTER
15 1:25 AM UT
8:25 PM EST
7:25 PM CST
6:25 PM MST
5:25 PM PST

NEW MOON
22 2:37 PM UT
9:37 AM EST
8:37 AM CST
7:37 AM MST
6:37 AM PST

FIRST QUARTER
30 7:41 PM UT
2:41 PM EST
1:41 PM CST
12:41 PM MST
11:41 AM PST

Daylight Saving Time begins March 11, add one hour where in effect.

4

NEW MOON	FIRST QUARTER	FULL MOON	LAST QUARTER	

		6 7:19 PM UT	13 10:50 AM UT	
		2:19 PM EST	5:50 AM EST	
		1:19 PM CST	4:50 AM CST	**APRIL**
		12:19 PM MST	3:50 AM MST	
		11:19 AM PST	2:50 AM PST	
		EGG MOON		
21 7:18 AM UT	29 9:57 AM UT	6 3:35 AM UT	12 9:47 PM UT	
2:18 AM EST	4:57 AM EST	5 10:35 PM EST	4:47 PM EST	
1:18 AM CST	3:57 AM CST	9:35 PM CST	3:47 PM CST	**MAY**
12:18 AM MST	2:57 AM MST	8:35 PM MST	2:47 PM MST	
20 11:18 PM PST	1:57 AM PST	7:35 PM PST	1:47 PM PST	
		MILK MOON		
20 11:47 PM UT	28 8:16 PM UT	4 11:12 AM UT	11 10:41 AM UT	
6:47 PM EST	3:16 PM EST	6:12 AM EST	5:41 AM EST	
5:47 PM CST	2:16 PM CST	5:12 AM CST	4:41 AM CST	
4:47 PM MST	1:16 PM MST	4:12 AM MST	3:41 AM MST	
3:47 PM PST	12:16 PM PST	3:12 AM PST	2:41 AM PST	**JUNE**
		ROSE MOON		
19 3:02 PM UT	27 3:30 AM UT			
10:02 AM EST	26 10:30 PM EST			
9:02 AM CST	9:30 PM CST			
8:02 AM MST	8:30 PM MST			
7:02 AM PST	7:30 PM PST			

• 2012 •
MOON PHASES

• FULL MOON HISTORY •

MAY 19, 1962 Marilyn Monroe serenaded John F. Kennedy by singing her version of "Happy Birthday, Mr. President" during a birthday party at Madison Square Garden.

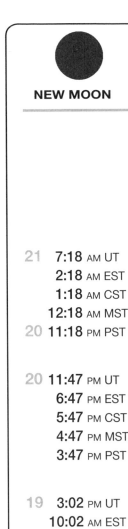

JUNE 5, 1955 On the highway between Hope, Arkansas, and Texarkana, Texas, Elvis Presley's first pink cadillac (a 1954 model), was destroyed by fire. On another full moon the same year (September 2), band member Scotty Moore was also involved in a car accident.

SUMMER SOLSTICE		
June 20	11:09 PM UT	
	6:09 PM EST	
	5:09 PM CST	
	4:09 PM MST	
	3:09 PM PST	

5

• 2012 •
MOON PHASES

	NEW MOON	FIRST QUARTER	FULL MOON	LAST QUARTER

6

FALL EQUINOX	
September 22	2:49 PM UT
	9:49 AM EST
	8:49 AM CST
	7:49 AM MST
	6:49 AM PST

JULY

	NEW MOON	FIRST QUARTER	FULL MOON	LAST QUARTER
			3 6:52 PM UT	11 1:48 AM UT
			1:52 PM EST	10 8:48 PM EST
			12:52 PM CST	7:48 PM CST
			11:52 AM MST	6:48 PM MST
			10:52 AM PST	5:48 PM PST
			BUCK MOON	
	19 4:24 AM UT	26 8:56 AM UT	2 3:27 AM UT	9 6:55 PM UT
	11:24 PM EST	3:56 AM EST	1 10:27 PM EST	1:55 PM EST
	10:24 PM CST	2:56 AM CST	9:27 PM CST	12:55 PM CST
	9:24 PM MST	1:56 AM MST	8:27 PM MST	11:55 AM MST
	8:24 PM PST	12:56 AM PST	7:27 PM PST	10:55 AM PST
			DOG DAYS MOON	

AUGUST

	NEW MOON	FIRST QUARTER	FULL MOON	LAST QUARTER
	17 3:54 PM UT	24 1:54 PM UT	31 1:58 PM UT	8 1:15 PM UT
	10:54 AM EST	8:54 AM EST	8:58 AM EST	8:15 AM EST
	9:54 AM CST	7:54 AM CST	7:58 AM CST	7:15 AM CST
	8:54 AM MST	6:54 AM MST	6:58 AM MST	6:15 AM MST
	7:54 AM PST	5:54 AM PST	5:58 AM PST	5:15 AM PST
			CORN MOON	

SEPTEMBER

	NEW MOON	FIRST QUARTER	FULL MOON	LAST QUARTER
	16 2:11 AM UT	22 7:41 PM UT	30 3:19 AM UT	
	15 9:11 PM EST	2:41 PM EST	29 10:19 PM EST	
	8:11 PM CST	1:41 PM CST	9:19 PM CST	
	7:11 PM MST	12:41 PM MST	8:19 PM MST	
	6:11 PM PST	11:41 AM PST	7:19 PM PST	
			HARVEST MOON	

NEW MOON	FIRST QUARTER	FULL MOON	LAST QUARTER

• 2012 • MOON PHASES

NEW MOON	FIRST QUARTER	FULL MOON	LAST QUARTER	
			8 7:33 AM UT	
			2:33 AM EST	
			1:33 AM CST	**OCTOBER**
			12:33 AM MST	
			7 11:33 PM PST	
15 12:03 PM UT	22 3:32 AM UT	29 7:49 PM UT	7 12:36 AM UT	
7:03 AM EST	10:32 PM EST	2:49 PM EST	6 7:36 PM EST	
6:03 AM CST	9:32 PM CST	1:49 PM CST	6:36 PM CST	**NOVEMBER**
5:03 AM MST	8:32 PM MST	12:49 PM MST	5:36 PM MST	
4:03 AM PST	7:32 PM PST	11:49 AM PST	4:36 PM PST	
		HUNTER'S MOON		

Daylight Saving Time ends November 4, clocks roll back one hour where in effect.

NEW MOON	FIRST QUARTER	FULL MOON	LAST QUARTER	
13 10:08 PM UT	20 2:31 PM UT	28 2:46 PM UT	6 3:31 PM UT	
5:08 PM EST	9:31 AM EST	9:46 AM EST	10:31 AM EST	
4:08 PM CST	8:31 AM CST	8:46 AM CST	9:31 AM CST	
3:08 PM MST	7:31 AM MST	7:46 AM MST	8:31 AM MST	
2:08 PM PST	6:31 AM PST	6:46 AM PST	7:31 AM PST	
		BEAVER MOON		**DECEMBER**
13 8:42 AM UT	20 5:19 AM UT	28 10:21 AM UT		
3:42 AM EST	12:19 AM EST	5:21 AM EST		
2:42 AM CST	19 11:19 PM CST	4:21 AM CST		
1:42 AM MST	10:19 PM MST	3:21 AM MST		
12:42 AM PST	9:19 PM PST	2:21 AM PST		
		COLD MOON		

• FULL MOON HISTORY •

NOVEMBER 12, 1799 Andrew Ellicott Douglass, an American astronomer, produced the first known record of a meteor shower in North America, the Leonids. In his journal, he wrote that the "whole heaven appeared as if illuminated with sky rockets, flying in an infinity of directions . . ."

NOVEMBER 13, 1875 Harvard and Yale Universities held their first football game on this date. The confrontation took place in New Haven; Harvard won 4-0.

WINTER SOLSTICE	
December 21	11:12 AM UT
	6:12 AM EST
	5:12 AM CST
	4:12 AM MST
	3:12 AM PST

7

OLD MARINER'S MOON TRANSIT RULE OF THUMB

A rough estimate of the Moon's transit can be figured (to within about an hour, not including Daylight Saving Time) with this method:

1. Start with the Moon's age in days.

2. Multiply the age by 4.

3. Divide the product by 5.

4. The whole part of the answer (the number to the left of the decimal point) is the hours past noon if 12 or less. If greater than 12, subtract 12 to get hours past midnight.

5. The remainder (the number to the right of the decimal point) is multiplied by 12 to produce the minutes past the hour (if larger than 60, adjust the quotient accordingly).

EXAMPLE

1. Moon's age is 11 days.

2. 11 x 4 = 44

3. 44 ÷ 5 = 8.8

4. Hours = 8 PM

5. Minutes = 8 x 12 = 48

Moon transits at about 8:48 PM.

• MOON HORIZONS •

The Moon follows roughly the same path as the Sun across the sky—a virtual line known as the ecliptic. Because of the ecliptic's tilt relative to the Earth, the Moon appears to rise at different points along the horizon from night to night and season to season. This point varies according to location, especially between cities far apart from north to south.

The chart opposite shows rising and setting points of the full moon for representative U.S. cities, measured by the azimuth (horizontal point on the horizon). North is 0 degrees, East is 90 degrees, South is 180 degrees, and West is 270 degrees (as illustrated at right). Imaginary lines rising from these points reach up to the zenith, the point directly overhead.

Once above the horizon, the Moon transits overhead across the local meridian, a virtual line running from north to south. The meridian marks the halfway point between the east and west horizons, and, because the Moon is always to the south at the point when it transits, traditional almanacs called this the Moon's "southing" or "moon up."

The moon's transit is different for every location—it crosses over New York City at a different time than it crosses over Cincinnati. The transit at any given spot is about 49 minutes later every day.

The only two constants that are easy to figure out about the transit are during the new moon and the full moon. At new moon, the Moon is directly in line with the Sun—the transit at this phase is the same as the Sun's, about midday. At full moon, the Moon is opposite the sun—the transit at this phase is about halfway through the night.

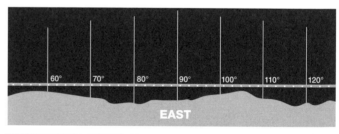

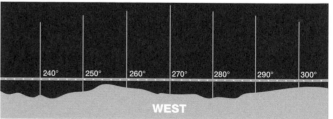

• FULL MOON RISE AND SET HORIZON LOCATOR •

		JAN 9	FEB 7	MAR 8	APR 6	MAY 5	JUN 4	JUL 3	AUG 1	AUG 31	SEP 29	OCT 29	NOV 28	DEC 28
Atlanta	RISE	69°	77°	94°	104°	112°	116°	113°	107°	92°	83°	71°	65°	67°
	SET	293°	285°	269°	259°	251°	243°	245°	251°	265°	274°	287°	295°	294°
Boston	RISE	66°	75°	94°	105°	114°	120°	116°	109°	93°	83°	69°	61°	64°
	SET	296°	287°	270°	258°	249°	240°	241°	248°	264°	274°	289°	298°	297°
Chicago	RISE	67°	76°	95°	106°	114°	120°	116°	109°	92°	82°	69°	62°	64°
	SET	295°	287°	269°	258°	249°	240°	242°	248°	264°	275°	289°	298°	297°
Columbus	RISE	67°	76°	94°	105°	114°	119°	115°	108°	93°	83°	69°	63°	65°
	SET	295°	287°	269°	259°	249°	241°	243°	249°	264°	274°	289°	297°	296°
Dallas	RISE	70°	78°	94°	104°	112°	116°	113°	106°	92°	83°	71°	65°	67°
	SET	292°	285°	269°	259°	251°	244°	245°	251°	265°	274°	287°	294°	293°
Denver	RISE	68°	77°	95°	105°	114°	119°	115°	108°	92°	82°	69°	63°	65°
	SET	294°	286°	269°	258°	249°	241°	243°	249°	265°	275°	289°	297°	296°
Miami	RISE	71°	78°	94°	103°	110°	114°	111°	105°	92°	84°	73°	67°	69°
	SET	291°	284°	270°	260°	252°	246°	247°	252°	265°	274°	286°	293°	292°
Los Angeles	RISE	69°	78°	95°	104°	112°	116°	113°	106°	92°	83°	71°	65°	67°
	SET	292°	285°	269°	259°	250°	243°	245°	251°	265°	275°	288°	295°	294°
Nashville	RISE	68°	77°	94°	104°	112°	117°	114°	107°	92°	83°	70°	64°	66°
	SET	293°	286°	269°	259°	250°	243°	244°	250°	265°	274°	288°	295°	295°
New York City	RISE	67°	76°	94°	105°	114°	119°	116°	109°	93°	83°	69°	62°	65°
	SET	295°	287°	270°	259°	249°	241°	242°	248°	265°	274°	289°	297°	296°
Phoenix	RISE	70°	78°	95°	104°	112°	116°	113°	106°	92°	83°	71°	65°	67°
	SET	292°	285°	269°	259°	251°	244°	245°	251°	265°	275°	288°	295°	294°
Salt Lake City	RISE	67°	76°	95°	106°	114°	119°	115°	108°	92°	82°	69°	62°	65°
	SET	295°	286°	269°	258°	249°	241°	243°	249°	265°	275°	289°	297°	296°
San Francisco	RISE	68°	77°	95°	105°	113°	118°	114°	107°	92°	82°	70°	63°	66°
	SET	293°	286°	269°	258°	249°	242°	244°	250°	265°	275°	289°	296°	295°
Seattle	RISE	64°	75°	96°	108°	118°	123°	119°	110°	92°	81°	66°	58°	62°
	SET	298°	288°	269°	256°	246°	237°	239°	246°	264°	276°	292°	301°	300°
Washington, DC	RISE	68°	76°	94°	105°	113°	118°	115°	108°	93°	83°	70°	63°	65°
	SET	294°	286°	269°	259°	250°	242°	243°	249°	264°	274°	288°	296°	296°

• MOON HEIGHT •

The Moon closely follows the ecliptic, the same path that the Sun appears to take across the sky. This path is tilted relative to the Earth's axis, making the height of the Sun and Moon vary throughout the year. During a full moon, when the Moon is opposite the Sun, it will appear high in the sky when the Sun is low, and vice versa.

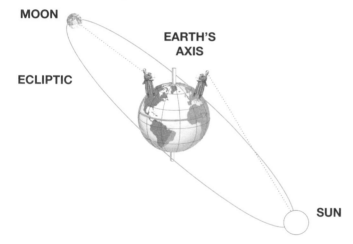

MOON

EARTH'S AXIS

ECLIPTIC

SUN

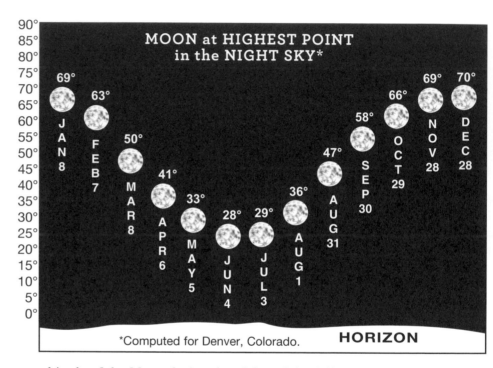

MOON at HIGHEST POINT in the NIGHT SKY*

JAN 8 — 69°
FEB 7 — 63°
MAR 8 — 50°
APR 6 — 41°
MAY 5 — 33°
JUN 4 — 28°
JUL 3 — 29°
AUG 1 — 36°
AUG 31 — 47°
SEP 30 — 58°
OCT 29 — 66°
NOV 28 — 69°
DEC 28 — 70°

*Computed for Denver, Colorado.   **HORIZON**

In a 24-hour period, as the Earth rotates into a different position relative to the ecliptic, an observer will see a marked difference in height between the Sun and the Moon when they are in opposition. This recurring pattern varies a bit because the Moon's path "wanders" back and forth across the ecliptic. When the two coincide during a full or new moon, the result is an eclipse.

The apparent altitude of the Moon varies according to an observer's location. The chart on the right indicates the peak altitude of the Moon during the nights of the full moons in 2012. During a full moon, which occurs halfway between moon rise and moon set, this point occurs about midnight.

The time and the actual altitude vary according to longitude and latitude (the figures used on this page are computed for Denver, Colorado). To find an exact altitude for the Moon for any day and location, see the altitude and azimuth calculator provided by the U.S. Naval Observatory (www.usno.navy.mil/USNO/astronomical-applications/data-services/alt-az-us).

10

At several times throughout the year, during the new moon, the Moon is not only close to the Sun, but it overlaps the Sun's position, producing a solar eclipse. Other than during eclipses, the new moon is too close to the Sun to be seen during the new moon—sunlight obscures it.

But every day after the new moon, the position of the Moon moves about 13 degrees farther away from the Sun. Within a few days after the new moon, the Sun sets, and the sky begins to darken while the first crescent of the Moon is above the horizon, producing a highly noticeable sight in the western sky.

For millenia, the point in time when this first crescent moon can be seen with the naked eye marked the beginning of a new lunar month. The Islamic religion still depends on the sighting of the first crescent moon to officially begin a monthly calendar cycle.

With the aid of computers and hundreds of years of experience, the prediction of when the first crescent moon can be seen has become more exact, but complex factors keep this from being a certainty.

Factors affecting the visibility of a young moon include the presence of obstructions on the local horizon (e.g. hills, mountains, trees), clouds or haze, the position of the Moon relative to the Sun (high or low relative to the ecliptic), and the time of year (the angle between the ecliptic and the horizon varies from season to season). Latitude and altitude are also factors; locations in lower latitudes favor an earlier sighting, as do higher altitudes.

At best, human observers without the use of binoculars, telescopes, or solar filters have been able to see a first crescent moon when it is only about fifteen hours "old"—fifteen hours after the exact time of the new moon. Most of the time, casual observers do not see an early crescent moon until two or more days after the new moon.

The potential to see any first crescent moon when it is less than twenty-four hours old is not great. Only at a few times during the year does the new moon occur at the right time, producing an optimal viewing "window" just after the following sunset, and, as often as not, clouds get in the way.

The prime conditions for first crescent observation occur when the Moon is closest to Earth (at the perigee of its orbit) near the time of the new moon, during the spring months, when the ecliptic is at its steepest angle relative to the horizon at sunset.

This first crescent moon is remarkably thin, yet it is twenty-eight hours old, seen the day after the new moon. It is far from the record for the youngest that has been observed.

• SKY SIGHTS NEAR THE MOON IN 2012 •

The following key dates represent prime viewing times for the Moon near the visible planets and major stars. Times are noted for the closest proximity, some of which may not be visible in the United States because of the differences in time zones. Graphics represent approximate positions projected in advance by Stellarium, an online planetarium program: **www.stellarium.com**

JANUARY

3 Jupiter 5° below the Moon (3 AM UT).

14 Waning moon rises with Mars above.

16 Saturn 6° left of the Moon (7 PM UT).

26 Young crescent moon sets with Venus above and left.

FEBRUARY

10 Mars high above the Moon.

13 Saturn 6° above the Moon (1 AM UT).

23 Young crescent moon sets with Venus high above.

25 Venus 3° below the Moon (10 PM UT).

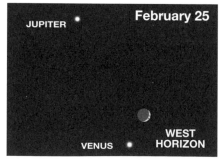

27 Jupiter 4° above the Moon (6 AM UT).

MARCH

8 Moon rises with Mars high above.

11 Saturn 6° above the Moon (7 AM UT).

26 Young crescent moon sets with Jupiter 3° below and Venus less than 2° right.

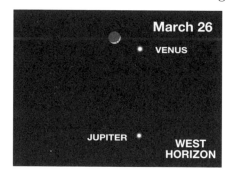

APRIL

3 Mars high above the Moon.

7 Full moon rises with Saturn 6° above.

22 Jupiter 2° below the Moon (7 PM UT).

24 Young crescent moon sets with Jupiter and Venus nearby.

30 Venus at greatest illumination.

MAY

1 Mars 8° above the Moon (2 PM UT).

4 Saturn 6° above the Moon (10 PM UT).

22 Very young crescent moon sets with Venus 5° above right.

29 Mars 7° above the Moon (11 AM UT).

JUNE

1 Saturn 7° above the Moon (5 AM UT).

17 Before sunrise in the eastern sky, Jupiter and Venus close to the Moon. Jupiter 1° below the Moon (8 AM UT).

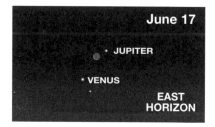

18 Venus 2° below the Moon (1 AM UT).

26 Mars 6° above the Moon (3 PM UT).

28 Saturn 6° above the Moon (12 PM UT).

JULY

12 Venus at greatest illumination.

14 Early in the morning, the Moon rises with Jupiter and Venus close (Jupiter closest), along with the bright star Aldebaran.

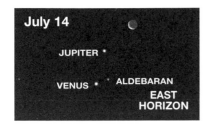

July 14

JUPITER

VENUS · ALDEBARAN

EAST HORIZON

15 Jupiter less than 1° from the Moon (3 AM UT).

23 Young crescent moon sets with Mars, Saturn, and the bright star Spica nearby.

· SATURN July 23

SPICA · MARS

WEST HORIZON

24 Mars 4° above the Moon (10 PM UT); Saturn high above.

25 Spica about 1° right of the Moon (5 PM UT); Saturn 6° above right (7 PM UT); Mars far right.

AUGUST

11 Jupiter less than 1° from the Moon (9 PM UT).

13 The Moon occults Venus in late afternoon, beginning not visible in the United States without special eye protection (8 PM UT).

20 Young crescent moon sets with Spica, Mars, and Saturn nearby.

21 Spica 1° to right of the Moon (10 PM UT).

22 Saturn 5° above the Moon (3 AM UT). Mars 2° above the Moon (8 AM UT).

SEPTEMBER

8 Jupiter less than 1° from the Moon (11 AM UT).

12 Venus 4° above the Moon (5 PM UT).

18 Young crescent moon sets with Spica, Mars, and Saturn nearby. Spica less than 1° from the Moon (5 AM UT).

19 Mars less than 1° from the Moon (9 PM UT).

OCTOBER

5 Jupiter less than 1° from the Moon (9 PM UT).

12 Venus 6° above the Moon (7 PM UT).

18 Mars 2° below the setting Moon (1 PM UT).

19 Young crescent moon sets with Mars and the bright star Antares nearby.

NOVEMBER

1 Moon sets with Jupiter close.

2 Jupiter less than 1° from the Moon (1 AM UT).

11 Moon rises with Spica, Saturn, and Venus nearby. Venus 5° from the Moon (6 PM UT).

1° 5° 10°

Use your fingers or hand to approximate distance measurements. The little finger at the end of an outstretched arm equals about 1 degree (about twice the angular diameter of the Moon or Sun). When spread (in the standard "V" sign), the index and middle fingers span about 5 degrees. A fist (or width of the hand) equals about 10 degrees.

12 Spica less than 1° from the Moon (2 AM UT). Saturn 4° from the Moon (9 PM UT).

16 Mars 4° from the Moon (10 AM UT).

29 Moon rises with Jupiter less than 1° away. (1 AM UT).

DECEMBER

9 Spica less than 1° from the Moon (12 PM UT).

10 Saturn 4° above the Moon (12 PM UT).

11 Venus less than 2° from the Moon (2 PM UT).

15 Young crescent moon sets with Mars 6° below (10 AM UT).

25 Moon rises with Jupiter very close. Jupiter less than 1° from the Moon (12 PM UT).

• MOON RISE and MOON SET •

		JANUARY				FEBRUARY			MARCH		
Atlanta	RISE	1 12:18 PM	9 6:29 PM	16 12:55 AM	30 11:22 AM	29 11:19 AM	7 6:21 PM	14 1:02 AM	30 2:45 PM	8 7:21 PM	14 2:01 AM
	SET	12:48 AM	7:45 AM	12:55 AM	12:26 AM	12:59 AM	7:00 AM	11:32 AM	2:20 AM	6:43 AM	12:18 PM
Boston	RISE	1 11:13 AM	9 5:15 PM	16 12:13 AM	30 10:11 AM	29 10:00 AM	7 5:14 PM	14 12:27 AM	30 1:27 AM	8 6:28 PM	14 1:30 AM
	SET	12:01 AM	7:10 AM	10:51 AM	—	12:27 AM	6:18 AM	10:15 AM	1:48 AM	5:48 AM	10:58 AM
Chicago	RISE	1 11:22 AM	9 5:25 PM	16 12:22 AM	30 10:20 AM	29 10:10 AM	7 5:24 PM	14 12:35 AM	30 11:38 AM	8 6:38 PM	14 1:38 AM
	SET	12:09 AM	7:17 AM	11:00 AM	—	12:34 AM	6:25 AM	10:25 AM	1:55 AM	5:56 AM	11:09 AM
Columbus	RISE	1 12:05 PM	9 6:10 PM	16 12:59 AM	30 11:05 AM	29 10:56 AM	7 6:07 PM	14 1:10 AM	30 12:24 PM	8 7:17 PM	14 2:12 AM
	SET	12:48 AM	7:53 AM	11:44 AM	12:31 AM	1:09 AM	7:03 AM	11:11 AM	2:30 AM	6:37 AM	11:55 AM
Dallas	RISE	1 12:10 PM	9 6:22 PM	16 12:45 AM	30 11:15 AM	29 11:12 AM	7 6:14 PM	14 12:51 AM	30 12:39 PM	8 7:12 PM	14 1:50 AM
	SET	12:38 AM	7:34 AM	11:54 AM	12:16 AM	12:48 AM	6:49 AM	11:26 AM	2:09 AM	6:34 AM	12:12 PM
Denver	RISE	1 10:35 AM	9 5:42 PM	16 12:31 AM		29 10:28 AM	7 5:40 PM	14 12:42 AM	30 1:56 AM	8 6:50 PM	14 1:43 AM
	SET	12:02 AM	7:23 AM	11:15 AM		12:40 AM	6:33 AM	10:42 AM	2:00 AM	6:07 AM	11:28 AM
Miami	RISE	1 12:09 PM	9 6:25 PM	16 12:27 AM	30 11:18 AM	29 11:19 AM	7 6:12 PM	14 12:28 AM	30 2:44 PM	8 7:01 PM	14 1:25 AM
	SET	12:24 AM	7:13 AM	11:56 AM	—	12:24 AM	6:32 AM	11:32 AM	1:46 AM	6:26 AM	12:19 PM
Nashville	RISE	1 11:25 AM	9 5:34 PM	16 12:08 AM	30 10:28 AM	29 10:22 AM	7 5:26 PM	14 12:17 AM	30 11:49 AM	8 6:32 PM	14 1:17 AM
	SET	12:00 PM	7:00 AM	11:07 AM	—	12:15 AM	6:13 AM	10:36 AM	1:36 AM	5:53 AM	11:22 AM
Los Angeles	RISE	1 11:16 AM	8 4:48 PM	16 12:18 AM	30 10:41 AM	29 10:38 AM	7 5:43 PM	14 12:24 AM	30 12:05 PM	8 6:43 PM	14 1:23 AM
	SET	12:43 AM	6:22 AM	11:20 AM	—	12:21 AM	6:19 AM	10:52 AM	1:41 AM	6:02 AM	11:39 AM
New York City	RISE	1 11:27 AM	9 5:30 PM	15 —	30 10:26 AM	29 10:17 AM	7 5:28 PM	14 12:34 AM	30 11:44 AM	8 6:40 PM	14 1:37 AM
	SET	12:11 AM	7:18 AM	10:31 AM	—	12:34 AM	6:27 AM	10:31 AM	1:55 AM	6:00 AM	11:15 AM
Phoenix	RISE		9 6:25 PM	16 12:51 AM	30 11:16 AM	29 11:14 AM	7 6:17 PM	14 12:57 AM	30 1:41 AM	8 7:17 PM	14 12:56 AM
	SET		7:39 AM	11:56 AM	12:21 AM	12:53 AM	6:53 AM	11:28 AM	1:14 AM	6:37 AM	11:14 AM
Salt Lake City	RISE		9 6:09 PM	16 1:01 AM	30 11:01 AM	29 10:53 AM	7 6:07 PM	14 1:14 AM	30 12:21 PM	8 7:19 PM	14 2:15 AM
	SET		7:54 AM	11:42 AM	12:33 AM	1:12 AM	7:02 AM	11:08 AM	2:32 AM	6:35 AM	11:53 AM
San Francisco	RISE		8 4:56 PM	16 12:40 AM	30 10:51 AM	29 10:45 AM	7 5:55 PM	14 12:50 AM	30 12:13 PM	8 7:02 PM	14 1:50 AM
	SET		6:48 AM	11:31 AM	12:11 AM	12:47 AM	6:41 PM	11:00 AM	2:07 AM	6:19 AM	11:46 AM
Seattle	RISE		8 4:26 PM	16 12:59 AM	30 10:27 AM	29 10:12 AM	7 5:41 PM	14 1:19 AM	30 11:43 AM	8 7:07 PM	14 2:24 AM
	SET		7:18 AM	11:09 AM	12:32 AM	1:18 AM	6:57 AM	10:29 AM	2:38 AM	6:17 AM	11:12 AM
Washington, D.C.	RISE	1 11:42 AM	9 5:47 PM	16 12:32 AM	30 10:43 AM	29 10:35 AM	7 5:44 PM	14 12:43 AM	30 2:02 PM	8 6:52 PM	14 1:44 AM
	SET	12:22 AM	7:26 AM	11:22 AM	12:04 AM	12:42 AM	6:37 AM	10:49 AM	2:03 AM	6:13 AM	11:34 AM

		APRIL			MAY			JUNE		
		29	6	13	28	5	12	26	4	11
Atlanta	RISE	12:32 PM	7:17 PM	1:32 AM	12:30 PM	7:14 PM	12:49 AM	12:22 PM	8:14 PM	12:27 AM
	SET	1:20 AM	5:51 AM	12:17 PM	12:41 AM	5:06 AM	12:10 PM	—	5:32 AM	12:54 PM
Boston	RISE	11:23 AM	6:33 PM	12:25 AM	11:25 AM	6:38 PM	—	11:30 AM	7:43 PM	11:58 PM
	SET	12:39 AM	4:48 AM	2:01 PM	—	3:54 AM	1:02 PM	11:13 PM	4:12 AM	12:01 AM
Chicago	RISE	11:34 AM	6:42 PM	1:03 AM	11:34 AM	6:47 PM	12:14 AM	11:40 AM	7:51 PM	—
	SET	12:46 AM	4:56 AM	11:13 AM	—	4:04 AM	11:14 AM	11:21 PM	4:23 AM	12:10 PM
Columbus	RISE	12:17 PM	7:19 PM	1:40 AM	11:14 AM	7:22 PM	12:51 AM	12:19 PM	8:25 PM	12:21 PM
	SET	1:24 AM	5:39 AM	11:58 AM	12:48 AM	4:48 AM	11:57 AM	—	5:09 AM	12:50 PM
Dallas	RISE	12:24 PM	7:08 PM	1:21 AM	12:17 PM	7:05 PM	12:38 AM	12:13 PM	8:04 PM	12:17 AM
	SET	1:09 AM	5:43 AM	12:10 PM	12:20 AM	4:58 AM	12:03 PM	—	5:26 AM	12:45 PM
Denver	RISE	11:49 AM	6:52 PM	1:09 AM	11:48 AM	6:54 PM	12:21 AM	11:51 AM	7:56 PM	—
	SET	12:53 AM	5:09 AM	11:31 AM	—	4:19 AM	11:29 AM	11:34 PM	4:42 AM	12:21 PM
Miami	RISE	12:24 PM	6:50 PM	1:00 AM	12:10 PM	6:42 PM	12:22 AM	12:01 PM	7:39 PM	12:09 PM
	SET	12:51 AM	5:40 AM	12:13 PM	12:08 AM	5:01 AM	12:00 PM	—	5:33 AM	12:35 PM
Nashville	RISE	11:38 AM	6:30 PM	12:47 AM	11:33 AM	6:29 PM	12:01 AM	11:33 AM	7:30 PM	—
	SET	12:33 AM	4:58 AM	11:22 AM	—	4:11 AM	11:17 AM	11:22 PM	4:36 AM	12:05 PM
Los Angeles	RISE	11:53 AM	6:40 PM	12:52 AM	11:46 AM	6:38 PM	12:08 AM	11:44 AM	7:37 PM	—
	SET	12:39 AM	5:10 AM	11:38 AM	—	4:25 AM	11:31 AM	11:33 PM	4:53 AM	12:15 PM
New York City	RISE	11:38 AM	6:42 PM	1:04 AM	11:37 AM	6:46 PM	12:15 AM	11:41 AM	7:50 PM	—
	SET	12:48 AM	5:01 AM	11:18 AM	—	4:09 AM	11:18 AM	11:26 PM	4:29 AM	12:12 PM
Phoenix	RISE	12:27 PM	7:13 PM	1:25 AM	12:20 PM	7:10 PM	12:42 AM	12:17 PM	8:09 PM	12:20 AM
	SET	1:13 AM	5:45 AM	12:12 PM	12:23 AM	5:00 AM	12:06 PM	—	5:28 AM	12:49 PM
Salt Lake City	RISE	12:16 PM	7:22 PM	1:40 AM	12:16 PM	7:26 PM	12:51 AM	12:20 PM	8:28 PM	12:19 AM
	SET	1:23 AM	5:36 AM	11:57 AM	12:27 AM	4:46 AM	11:56 AM	—	5:07 AM	12:51 PM
San Francisco	RISE	12:05 PM	7:02 PM	1:17 AM	11:03 AM	5:49 PM	12:32 AM	12:03 PM	8:03 PM	12:02 AM
	SET	1:02 AM	5:23 AM	11:48 AM	12:25 AM	4:47 AM	10:43 AM	11:47 PM	5:00 AM	12:34 PM
Seattle	RISE	11:48 AM	7:19 PM	1:42 AM	11:56 AM	7:30 PM	12:45 AM	12:09 PM	8:36 PM	12:01 AM
	SET	1:19 AM	5:10 AM	11:23 AM	12:16 AM	4:12 AM	11:30 AM	11:36 PM	4:27 AM	12:37 PM
Washington, D.C.	RISE	11:54 AM	6:53 PM	1:12 AM	11:51 AM	6:55 PM	12:25 AM	11:53 AM	7:57 PM	—
	SET	12:57 AM	5:16 AM	11:35 AM	12:03 AM	4:26 AM	11:33 AM	11:40 PM	4:48 AM	12:25 PM

· MOON RISE AND MOON SET ·

		JULY					AUGUST					SEPTEMBER		
Atlanta	RISE	26	1:30 PM	3	7:49 PM	10	—	24	1:34 PM	1	7:10 PM	9	11:47 PM	31	6:54 PM	22	1:27 PM	29	5:59 PM	8	11:58 PM
	SET		—		5:22 AM		12:36 PM		11:58 PM		5:17 AM		1:11 PM		6:13 AM		11:54 PM		6:01 AM		1:37 PM
Boston	RISE	26	12:52 PM	3	7:15 PM	10	10:55 PM	24	1:01 PM	1	6:30 PM	9	10:32 PM	31	6:02 PM	22	12:55 PM	29	4:59 PM	8	10:40 PM
	SET		11:03 PM		4:03 AM		11:50 AM		10:39 PM		4:04 AM		12:35 PM		5:13 AM		10:36 PM		5:09 AM		1:05 PM
Chicago	RISE	26	12:01 PM	3	7:22 PM	10	11:03 PM	24	1:09 PM	1	6:37 PM	9	10:41 PM	31	6:09 PM	22	1:02 PM	29	5:07 PM	8	10:50 PM
	SET		11:12 PM		4:14 AM		11:59 AM		10:50 PM		4:15 AM		12:43 PM		5:23 AM		10:46 AM		5:18 AM		1:12 PM
Columbus	RISE	26	1:37 PM	3	7:58 PM	10	11:47 PM	24	1:44 PM	1	7:14 PM	9	11:27 PM	31	6:50 PM	22	1:37 PM	29	5:49 PM	8	11:36 PM
	SET		11:57 PM		5:00 AM		12:37 PM		11:36 PM		4:59 AM		1:19 PM		6:04 AM		11:32 PM		5:57 AM		1:47 PM
Dallas	RISE	26	1:20 PM	3	7:38 PM	10	11:52 PM	24	1:23 PM	1	7:00 PM	9	11:40 PM	31	6:45 PM	22	11:13 AM	29	5:50 PM	8	11:52 PM
	SET		—		5:16 AM		12:27 PM		11:52 PM		5:10 AM		1:00 PM		6:05 AM		10:10 PM		5:52 AM		1:26 PM
Denver	RISE	26	1:08 PM	3	7:28 PM	10	11:17 PM	24	1:15 PM	1	6:44 PM	9	10:58 PM	31	6:20 PM	22	1:07 PM	29	5:19 PM	8	11:08 PM
	SET		11:29 PM		4:33 AM		12:08 PM		11:08 PM		4:32 AM		12:49 PM		5:36 AM		11:05 PM		5:29 AM		1:18 PM
Miami	RISE	26	12:59 PM	3	7:16 PM	10	11:52 PM	24	12:59 PM	1	6:42 PM	9	11:45 PM	31	6:36 PM	22	12:52 PM	29	5:46 PM	8	11:58 PM
	SET		—		5:21 AM		12:11 PM		11:58 PM		5:12 AM		12:39 PM		5:59 AM		11:53 PM		5:41 AM		1:02 PM
Nashville	RISE	26	12:45 PM	3	7:50 PM	10	11:07 PM	24	12:50 PM	1	6:23 PM	9	10:52 PM	31	6:05 PM	22	12:42 PM	29	5:07 PM	8	11:02 PM
	SET		11:22 PM		4:26 AM		11:48 AM		11:02 PM		4:22 AM		12:26 PM		5:22 AM		10:58 PM		5:12 AM		12:53 PM
Los Angeles	RISE	26	12:53 PM	3	7:10 PM	10	11:19 PM	24	12:56 PM	1	6:30 PM	9	11:06 PM	31	6:13 PM	22	12:49 PM	29	5:17 PM	8	11:18 PM
	SET		11:36 PM		4:43 AM		11:57 AM		11:19 PM		4:39 AM		12:32 PM		5:34 AM		11:15 PM		5:22 AM		12:58 PM
New York City	RISE	26	1:00 PM	3	7:22 PM	10	11:08 PM	24	1:08 PM	1	6:38 PM	9	10:48 PM	31	6:13 PM	22	1:02 PM	29	5:11 PM	8	10:56 PM
	SET		11:18 PM		4:20 AM		12:00 PM		10:56 PM		4:19 AM		12:43 PM		5:26 AM		10:52 PM		5:20 AM		1:12 PM
Phoenix	RISE	26	1:25 PM	3	7:43 PM	10	11:54 PM	24	1:29 PM	1	7:04 PM	9	11:42 PM	31	6:48 PM	22	1:21 PM	29	5:52 PM	8	11:53 PM
	SET		—		5:18 AM		12:31 PM		11:54 PM		5:13 AM		1:05 PM		6:08 AM		11:50 PM		5:56 AM		1:31 PM
Salt Lake City	RISE	26	1:40 PM	3	7:59 PM	10	11:43 PM	24	1:47 PM	1	7:14 PM	9	11:24 PM	31	6:48 PM	22	1:39 PM	29	5:46 PM	8	11:33 PM
	SET		11:55 PM		4:59 AM		12:38 PM		11:34 PM		4:58 AM		1:21 PM		6:04 AM		11:31 PM		5:58 AM		1:49 PM
San Francisco	RISE	26	1:17 PM	3	7:36 PM	10	11:31 PM	24	1:23 PM	1	6:53 PM	9	11:15 PM	31	6:31 PM	22	1:15 PM	29	5:32 PM	8	11:26 PM
	SET		11:45 PM		4:51 AM		12:19 PM		11:26 PM		4:49 AM		12:57 PM		5:50 AM		11:23 PM		5:41 AM		1:24 PM
Seattle	RISE	26	1:42 PM	3	8:03 PM	10	11:14 PM	24	1:54 PM	1	7:10 PM	9	10:46 PM	31	6:32 PM	22	1:45 PM	29	5:23 PM	8	10:54 PM
	SET		11:18 PM		4:20 AM		12:32 PM		10:53 PM		4:26 AM		1:24 PM		5:44 AM		10:52 PM		5:46 AM		1:56 PM
Washington, D.C.	RISE	26	1:09 PM	3	7:31 PM	10	11:24 PM	24	1:16 PM	1	6:48 PM	9	11:05 PM	31	6:25 PM	22	1:09 PM	29	5:25 PM	8	11:14 PM
	SET		11:35 PM		4:38 AM		12:11 PM		11:14 PM		4:36 AM		12:51 PM		5:40 AM		11:10 PM		5:32 AM		1:20 PM

16

		OCTOBER						NOVEMBER						DECEMBER					
Atlanta	RISE	22	1:44 PM	29	5:41 PM	8	—	20	12:58 PM	28	5:44 PM	6	—	20	12:36 PM	28	6:11 PM	6	12:03 AM
	SET		—		6:43 AM		1:44 PM		—		7:19 PM		12:56 PM		12:39 AM		7:38 AM		12:37 PM
Boston	RISE	22	12:04 PM	29	4:30 PM	8	11:18 PM	20	12:10 PM	28	4:26 PM	6	11:09 PM	20	11:37 AM	28	4:55 PM	6	—
	SET		11:49 PM		6:03 AM		1:07 PM		11:51 AM		6:46 AM		12:14 PM		—		7:04 AM		11:43 AM
Chicago	RISE	22	1:11 PM	29	4:39 PM	8	11:28 PM	20	12:17 PM	28	4:36 PM	6	11:19 PM	19	11:16 AM	28	5:05 PM	6	—
	SET		11:59 PM		6:11 AM		1:14 PM		—		6:53 AM		12:21 PM		11:56 PM		7:11 AM		11:51 AM
Columbus	RISE	22	1:48 PM	29	5:24 PM	8	—	20	12:56 PM	28	5:22 PM	6	—	20	12:27 PM	28	5:51 PM	6	—
	SET		—		6:48 AM		1:51 PM		—		7:28 AM		12:32 PM		12:35 AM		7:47 AM		12:32 PM
Dallas	RISE	22	1:34 PM	29	5:34 PM	8	—	20	12:48 PM	28	5:37 PM	6	—	19	11:55 AM	28	6:04 PM	6	—
	SET		—		6:33 AM		1:33 PM		—		7:08 AM		12:45 PM		—		7:27 AM		12:28 PM
Denver	RISE	22	1:18 PM	29	4:55 PM	8	11:45 PM	20	12:26 PM	28	4:54 PM	6	11:34 PM	19	11:27 AM	28	5:23 PM	6	—
	SET		—		6:19 AM		1:57 PM		—		6:59 AM		12:28 PM		—		7:17 AM		12:02 PM
Miami	RISE	22	1:16 PM	29	5:36 PM	8	—	20	12:36 PM	28	5:43 PM	6	—	20	12:24 PM	28	6:09 PM	6	—
	SET		—		6:14 AM		1:12 PM		—		6:45 AM		12:29 PM		12:19 AM		7:05 AM		12:19 PM
Nashville	RISE	22	12:58 PM	29	4:47 PM	8	10:55 PM	20	12:09 PM	28	4:48 PM	6	11:22 PM	19	11:14 AM	28	5:15 PM	6	—
	SET		—		5:57 AM		12:23 PM		—		5:34 AM		12:08 PM		11:50 PM		6:53 AM		11:47 AM
Los Angeles	RISE	22	1:04 PM	29	5:00 PM	7	10:55 PM	20	12:17 PM	28	5:03 PM	6	11:36 PM	19	11:23 AM	28	5:31 PM	6	—
	SET		—		6:05 AM		12:23 PM		—		6:40 AM		12:15 PM		—		6:58 AM		11:56 AM
New York City	RISE	22	1:12 PM	29	4:45 PM	8	11:34 PM	20	12:20 PM	28	4:43 PM	6	11:23 PM	20	11:49 AM	28	5:11 PM	6	—
	SET		—		6:11 AM		1:15 PM		—		6:53 AM		12:23 PM		—		7:12 AM		11:55 AM
Phoenix	RISE	22	1:38 PM	29	5:35 PM	8	—	20	12:51 PM	28	5:39 PM	6	—	19	11:57 AM	28	6:06 PM	6	—
	SET		—		6:38 AM		1:37 PM		—		7:13 AM		12:49 PM		—		7:31 AM		12:30 PM
Salt Lake City	RISE	22	1:48 PM	29	5:21 PM	8	—	20	12:55 PM	28	5:19 PM	6	—	19	11:55 AM	28	5:49 PM	6	—
	SET		—		6:49 AM		1:51 PM		—		7:30 AM		12:58 PM		—		7:48 AM		12:30 PM
San Francisco	RISE	22	1:27 PM	29	5:10 PM	7	11:04 PM	20	12:36 PM	28	5:11 PM	6	11:49 PM	19	11:39 AM	28	5:40 PM	6	—
	SET		—		6:28 AM		12:48 PM		—		7:06 AM		12:37 PM		—		7:24 AM		12:13 PM
Seattle	RISE	22	1:44 PM	29	4:47 PM	7	10:36 PM	20	12:43 PM	28	4:40 PM	6	11:35 PM	20	12:01 PM	28	5:12 PM	6	—
	SET		—		6:48 AM		1:16 PM		—		7:36 AM		12:52 PM		12:24 AM		7:52 AM		12:13 PM
Washington, D.C.	RISE	22	1:22 PM	29	5:02 PM	8	11:50 PM	20	12:31 PM	28	5:01 PM	6	11:38 PM	20	12:03 PM	28	5:29 PM	6	—
	SET		—		6:21 AM		1:24 PM		—		7:01 AM		12:33 PM		12:10 AM		7:20 AM		12:07 PM

• PARTIAL ECLIPSE OF THE MOON: JUNE 4 •

The entire eclipse will be visible throughout the United States, except for the beginning phase, which will only be visible in the Northeast.

A. BEGINS	8:47 AM	UT
	3:46 AM	EST
	2:46 AM	CST
	1:46 AM	MST
	12:46 AM	PST
B. MIDDLE	11:03 AM	UT
	6:03 AM	EST
	5:03 AM	CST
	4:03 AM	MST
	3:03 AM	PST
C. ENDS	1:20 PM	UT
	8:19 AM	EST
	7:19 AM	CST
	6:19 AM	MST
	5:19 AM	PST

ADD 1 HOUR FOR DAYLIGHT SAVING TIME.

N

C   B   A

ECLIPSE DIRECTION

ECLIPTIC

E   W

UMBRA

PENUMBRA

S

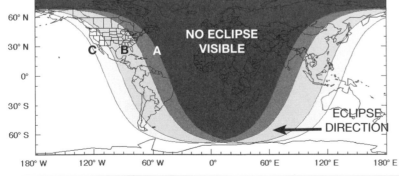

Note: These graphics are derived from originals produced by NASA and the U.S. Naval Observatory. For more detailed information, visit the Eclipse Portal provided by the U.S. Naval Observatory:

http://aa.usno.navy.mil/data/docs/UpcomingEclipses.php

• PENUMBRAL ECLIPSE OF THE MOON: NOVEMBER 28 •

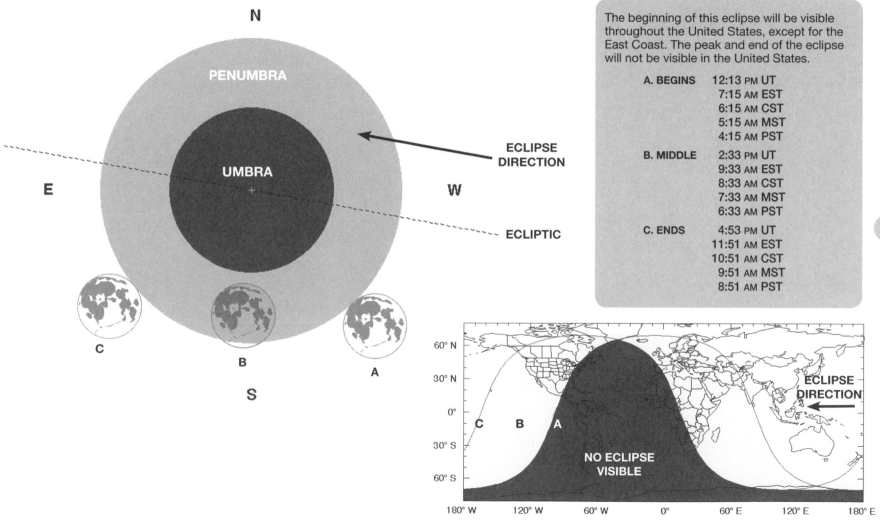

N

PENUMBRA

UMBRA

ECLIPSE DIRECTION

E

W

ECLIPTIC

C

B

A

S

The beginning of this eclipse will be visible throughout the United States, except for the East Coast. The peak and end of the eclipse will not be visible in the United States.

A. BEGINS	12:13 PM UT
	7:15 AM EST
	6:15 AM CST
	5:15 AM MST
	4:15 AM PST
B. MIDDLE	2:33 PM UT
	9:33 AM EST
	8:33 AM CST
	7:33 AM MST
	6:33 AM PST
C. ENDS	4:53 PM UT
	11:51 AM EST
	10:51 AM CST
	9:51 AM MST
	8:51 AM PST

60° N

30° N

0°

30° S

60° S

C   B   A

NO ECLIPSE VISIBLE

ECLIPSE DIRECTION

180° W   120° W   60° W   0°   60° E   120° E   180° E

• ANNULAR ECLIPSE OF THE SUN: MAY 20 •

An annular eclipse is one in which the Moon's diameter is not large enough to completely cover the Sun. This happens when the Moon is at a point on its elliptical path where it is farthest away from the Earth, reducing its apparent diameter. In such circumstances, at full eclipse, a ring of light is visible around the Moon.

The annular eclipse on May 20, 2012, will be visible in most of the United States. As the map on the right indicates, it will not be visible in the extreme eastern region.

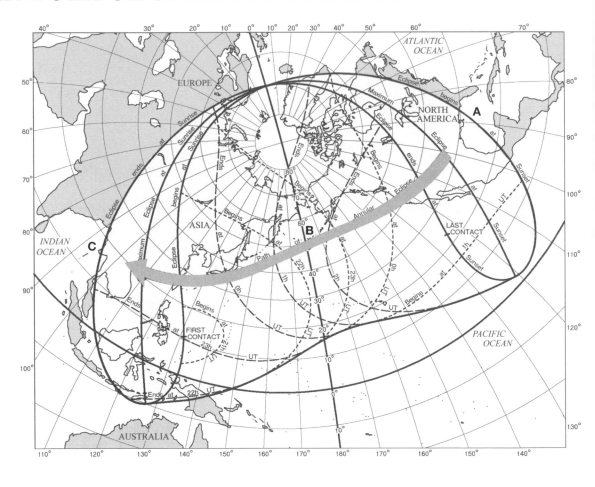

USE APPROVED FILTERS WHEN LOOKING AT THE SUN.

A. BEGINS	10:56 PM UT
	5:56 PM EST
	4:56 PM CST
	3:56 PM MST
	2:56 PM PST
B. MIDDLE	11:59 PM UT
	6:56 PM EST
	5:56 PM CST
	4:56 PM MST
	3:56 PM PST
C. ENDS	2:49 AM UT (May 21)
	9:49 PM EST
	8:56 PM CST
	7:56 PM MST
	6:56 PM PST

ADD 1 HOUR FOR DAYLIGHT SAVING TIME.

• TOTAL ECLIPSE OF THE SUN: NOVEMBER 13–14 •

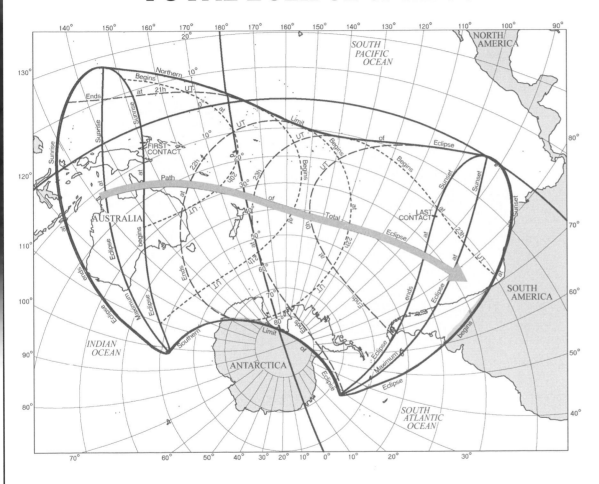

Eclipse graphics derived from maps by the Astronomical Applications Department, U.S. Naval Observatory.

NOT VISIBLE IN NORTH AMERICA

• FULL MOON HISTORY •

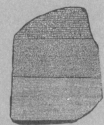

AUGUST 15, 1799 The Rosetta Stone, an artifact carved with ancient hieroglyphics (from 196 BC), was discovered in Egypt on this day in 1799 by French explorers. Its current home is the British Museum.

MAY 1, 1931 The Empire State Building in New York City was dedicated.

MAY 18, 1935 T.E. Lawrence, better known as "Lawrence of Arabia," died in a motorcycle accident near Dorset, England. He was 46 years old.

SEPTEMBER 28, 1939 Germany and the Soviet Union signed the "Friendship Treaty."

JUNE 6, 1944 Allied forces landed on the shores of Normandy, France, an event marked as D-Day in the European Theater during World War II.

• BLUE MOON: AUGUST 31 •

On the last day of August, the second full moon of the month will occur, a so-called "blue moon." In recent years, such an event has prompted media and public speculation, as such an occurrence does not happen every year.

The last blue moon was in December 2009. After 2012, the next blue moon is due in July 2015.

What's the significance? Only a quirk of the calendar—the occurrence has no significance in astronomy and very little from a cultural or religious perspective, except for curiosity.

More unusual for lunar cycles in 2012 is the lack of a first quarter moon in the month of February, at least in Europe. February, at a length of 28 or 29 days, has barely enough room to host the four quarter phases, and not enough time to span the entire lunar month of 29½ days. If a new moon or full moon happens to fall on the last day of January, the next new moon or full moon may skip February entirely.

In calendar terms, this is the rarest month of all—a February without a full moon. Such an event has happened only four times in the last century and will only happen four times in the current one, the next such event coming in 2018.

• THE MOON'S ILLUMINATION •

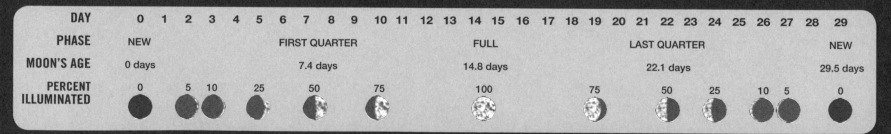

DAY	0	1	2	3	4	5	6	7	8	9	10	11	12	13	14	15	16	17	18	19	20	21	22	23	24	25	26	27	28	29
PHASE	NEW						FIRST QUARTER								FULL							LAST QUARTER								NEW
MOON'S AGE	0 days							7.4 days							14.8 days							22.1 days								29.5 days
PERCENT ILLUMINATED	0		5	10		25			50			75			100					75			50		25		10	5		0

• NAMES OF THE FULL MOONS •

January 8 (U.S. time zones) WINTER MOON or WOLF MOON First full moon after the winter solstice (or after Christmas). The Dakota Sioux called it the *Moon of the Terrible.*

February 7 SNOW MOON Second full moon of the year, associated with the middle of winter. Also called the *Trapper's Moon.* The Micmac tribe called it the *Snow-Blinding Moon.*

March 8 WORM MOON Last full moon before the spring equinox, when the first signs of warmer weather appear, or when the first worm castings are seen in the thawing earth. Colonists also called this the *Fish Moon* or the *Sap Moon.*

April 6 PLANTER'S MOON or EGG MOON First moon after the spring equinox, time for farmers to begin planting crops. The Algonquin called it the *Pink Moon,* referring to wild ground phlox (*phlox divaricata*), a native plant with a pink flower that bloomed during this time.

May 5 (U.S. time zones) MILK MOON or FLOWER MOON Fifth full moon of the year, corresponding to the season's first regular supply of milk as calves are weaned. The Lakota Sioux called this the *Moon of the Shedding Ponies.*

June 4 ROSE MOON By tradition, the full moon closest to the summer solstice (but not in 2012). Also called the *Strawberry Moon* and the *Honey Moon* for these seasonally available foods.

July 3 SUMMER MOON Associated with the middle of summer, after the summer solstice. Also called the *Buck Moon* for the time when new antlers appear on male deer.

August 1 (U.S. time zones) DOG DAYS MOON Associated with the rising of the star Sirius (the "dog" star) at sunrise, hence the name. Some colonists also called this the *Woodcutter's Moon* (time to begin gathering firewood for winter) or the *Sturgeon Moon.* In most years (but not 2012), the last full moon of summer.

August 31 CORN MOON The second full moon in August 2012 will be a Blue Moon, although this convention was not used until the twentieth century. Traditionally, this full moon would be the *Corn Moon.*

September 30 HARVEST MOON The full moon closest to the fall equinox (this year it is on September 22). At this time of year the moon rises at its steepest angle, seeming to linger near the horizon about the same time for several nights in a row, aiding farmers who worked long hours to harvest their crops. Also called the *Moon When the Calves Grow Hair* (Lakota Sioux).

October 29 HUNTER'S MOON The full moon following the Harvest Moon. Also called the *Blood Moon* (referring to the harvesting of livestock or game), the *Turkey's Moon* (Natchez), and *Falling of the Leaves Moon* (Ojibway).

November 28 BEAVER MOON Second full moon after the fall equinox (in some years, but not always), marking the season when beavers were fat and their pelts thick. Also called the *Freezing Moon* (Cheyenne).

December 28 CHRISTMAS MOON or COLD MOON Full moon closest to the winter solstice (in most years, before the solstice). Also called the *Long Night Moon* because the full moon rides high in the sky in this season.

• MOON HOLIDAYS •

The lunar calendar, based on the 29.5-day lunar month, has been in use far longer than our current civil calendar, and parallels the development of various solar calendars.

Lunar and lunisolar (a hybrid version combining elements of both lunar and solar years) calendar cultures include those of Mesopotamia, Babylon, ancient Egypt, ancient Greece, the Zoroastrian religion, the Chinese empire, ancient Celts, and others.

Some countries and a few religions still base their calendars on a lunar cycle, even though civil calendars may also be used. Islam and Judaism are among these. All of the Islamic countries use the official Muslim calendar that was first adopted in 634 AD; except for Orthodox sects, most Jews restrict their lunar observances to the major traditional holidays, where applicable.

Buddhists establish their new year with the lunar cycle, but variations abound. The first full moon in May is linked to the date of Buddha's Enlightenment and is the starting point of some of these calendars.

Countries that adhere to Mahayana Buddhism (including much of China, Mongolia, Japan, and Indonesia) celebrate their new year on the first full moon in January. Chinese New Year, the most familiar to Westerners, typically occurs between January 21 and February 21.

Hindus in some regions recognize Ugadi, the first day of the month of Chaitra, as the beginning of the new year. The first month of the lunar Hindu calendar, Chaitra begins with the new moon in March. In other regions, the occasion is recognized later, during the month of Vaisakha, which begins with the new moon in April. Other variations are common—scholars note at least thirty versions currently in use. In some, months are new moon to new moon; in others, full moon to full moon.

Here, in more detail, is how a few of these holidays relate to the lunar cycle:

• EASTER The date for Easter in the Christian religion is designated as the first Sunday that falls after the first full moon (traditionally called the *Pascal Full Moon*) occurring on or after the spring equinox. The earliest date for Easter is March 22; the latest date is April 25. Easter shares its origins with Passover,

and, because of the similarity in setting their dates, they often fall within about a week of each other. Occasionally, Passover can be as much as one month later. The standard for Gregorian Easter (observed by most Western Christians) differs from Julian Easter (observed by orthodox sects). The dates can vary by one to four weeks because

• 2012 HOLIDAYS •

CHINESE NEW YEAR	January 23
PERSIAN NEW YEAR	March 20
SAKA (Indian New Year)	March 21
UGADI (Hindu New Year)	March 23
BUDDHIST NEW YEAR (Theravadin)	April 6
FIRST DAY OF PASSOVER	April 7*
EASTER	April 8
SONGKRAN (Thai New Year)	April 13
WESAK (Buddha's Birthday)	May 5
FIRST DAY OF RAMADAN	July 20*
ROSH HASHANAH (Jewish New Year)	September 17*
MUHARRAM (Islamic New Year)	November 15*

* Begins at sunset on the previous evening

24

the calculations used by orthodox churches rely on the old Julian calendar, which was superceded by the Gregorian calendar in most of the Western world (in October 1582 AD).

- **MUHARRAM** Islam determines the start of its lunar-based calendar with the date the prophet emigrated from Mecca to Medina, (an event known as the Hijra), which was July 16, 622 AD on the Western calendar. In 2012, this day will be November 15. The first month of the Islamic calendar is Muharram; Al-Hijra Muharram is New Year's day. With all the Islamic lunar-based holidays, the dates move back from year to year until a thirty-two year (more or less) cycle matches them up once again with the Western calendar.

- **RAMADAN** Muslims mark the month in which the Quran was revealed to the prophet as their holiest holiday, Ramadan. This religious holiday begins with the sighting of the first crescent moon in the ninth month of the Muslim calendar, also known as Ramadan. The observances end with the sighting of the following crescent moon. The dates of the new moon marking Ramadan move backward relative to the civil calendar, by more than one week a year, synchronizing with the civil (solar) calendar about every thirty-two years.

- **ROSH HASHANAH** The first day of the month Tishrei in the Jewish calendar is celebrated as the Jewish New Year, Rosh Hashanah. It was originally marked by the first observance of the crescent moon, but visual evidence is no longer required. The date is adjusted according to when the new moon is calculated to occur—moving later by one or two days according to complex rules—and marked by a fixed number of days after the previous beginning of the year. Jewish year 5773 begins with Rosh Hashanah in 2012.

- **PASSOVER** Passover (Pesach) is the traditional Jewish holiday designated to commemorate the exodus of the Jews from Egypt. This event occurred at the beginning of spring, and the celebration of Passover is configured to correspond to a lunar month near the spring equinox. In the fourth century, a system was designed to reduce the variables affecting this date. Passover begins on the fifteenth day of the Jewish month of Nisan—halfway through the lunar month and at the time of a full moon. Nisan is the first month after the spring (vernal) equinox, which can occur in either March or April. The earliest date for the beginning of Passover is March 21; the latest is April 20.

Chinese immigrants brought a now-familiar festival to the United States: the Chinese New Year's parade.

Illustration from *The World: Its Cities and People* (London: Cassell &Co., c. 1880)

The major influence creating tides is the gravitational effect of the Moon. If it were only a simple interaction, a high tide would occur as the Moon was at the meridian of a given location, its point of transit. But complex interactions with other factors generate a lag before a high or low tide peaks. This lag is called the *lunitidal interval*.

There is an average lunitidal interval for every location—if this number is known, the time of high tide can be predicted by subtracting the interval from the known time of the Moon's meridian.

Factors affecting the tidal cycle include the Sun's gravity, underwater and shore topography, the depth of water, the size of the body of water, and the weather. Barometric pressure alone is enough to raise or lower sea level by a foot or more.

The two phases in the lunar cycle when tides are highest are the new moon and the full moon, when the gravitational forces of the Sun and Moon are aligned. These monthly high tides (and corresponding low tides) are called *spring tides* (from the German word *springen*—"to rise up"). The semi-high and -low tides that occur during the first and last quarter moons are called *neap tides* (from the Middle English word *neep* pertaining to such tides).

Extra-high tides called *perigean spring tides* occur during a full or new moon when the Moon is closest to the Earth in its orbit, at its perigee (if this is the closest perigee of the year, the event is called a *proxigean spring tide*). Most of the time, monthly perigees do not coincide with full or new moons, making this a relatively rare event, occurring about every one and a half years (the full or new moon has to occur within about five hours of the perigee to achieve the combined effect).

In the past 400 years, records show there were thirty-nine proxigean spring tides. Between 2000 and 2036, eight proxigean spring tides are predicted (*Journal of Coastal Research*, March 2007).

Spring tides are about 20 percent higher or lower than average tides. Proxigean spring tides are even higher, but the excess is not always predictable. Historical records show that proxigean spring tides have sometimes, but not always, brought coastal flooding. Even with normal tides, weather conditions can completely mask tidal peaks—highs and lows—and delay or accelerate predicted tides by up to an hour,

• MOTHER of ALL TIDES? •

A PROXIGEAN SPRING TIDE—a high tide that arrives when a full or new moon coincides with the closest point in the Moon's orbit—is on the way for May 5, 2012 (May 6 to the east of the United States). This event will occur at 11:34 PM Eastern Daylight Time (8:35 PM Pacific Daylight Time), but the times of local high tides will vary.

especially in coastal areas with relatively shallow water and sites inland.

The next predicted proxigean spring tide is due on May 5, 2012 (May 6 to the east of the United States). A long history of observations of tides and their effects suggests conservative expectations from this event. Offshore winds and storm surges usually create the most damage—regardless of any match-up with high tides. The expected higher-than-normal tide could be a record-setting calamity or, like many such previous events of this potential scale, turn out to be a dud.

Jan 1　1:15 AM EST
Jan 30 11:10 PM EST
Feb 29　8:21 PM EST
Mar 30　2:41 PM EST
Apr 29　4:57 AM EST

May 28　3:16 PM EST
Jun 26 10:30 PM EST
Aug 26　3:56 AM EST
Aug 24　8:54 AM EST
Sep 22　2:41 PM EST

Oct 22 10:32 PM EST
Nov 20　9:31 AM EST
Dec 20 12:19 AM EST

THE DAYS OF new moon and full moon—listed on the left—represent the days when the highest high and lowest low tides will occur.

For a given location, the time of day or night for these tides will be the time of the Moon's local transit minus the lunitidal interval for this location.

The most accurate times are to be found with location tide tables (in print or the online equivalent), or with special watches and clocks that can be set to produce these numbers.

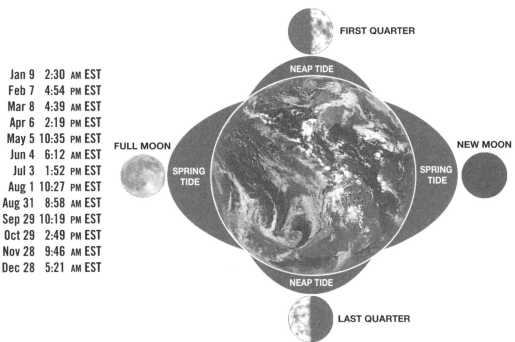

FIRST QUARTER

NEAP TIDE

FULL MOON

SPRING TIDE

NEW MOON

SPRING TIDE

NEAP TIDE

LAST QUARTER

Jan 9　2:30 AM EST
Feb 7　4:54 PM EST
Mar 8　4:39 AM EST
Apr 6　2:19 PM EST
May 5 10:35 PM EST
Jun 4　6:12 AM EST
Jul 3　1:52 PM EST
Aug 1 10:27 PM EST
Aug 31　8:58 AM EST
Sep 29 10:19 PM EST
Oct 29　2:49 PM EST
Nov 28　9:46 AM EST
Dec 28　5:21 AM EST

Jan 23　2:39 AM EST
Feb 21　5:35 PM EST
Mar 22　9:37 AM EST
Apr 21　2:18 AM EST
May 20　6:47 PM EST
Jun 19 10:02 AM EST
Jul 18 11:24 PM EST
Aug 17 10:54 AM EST
Sep 15　9:11 PM EST
Oct 15　7:03 AM EST
Nov 13　5:08 PM EST
Dec 13　3:42 AM EST

Jan 16　4:08 AM EST
Feb 14 12:04 PM EST
Mar 14　8:25 PM EST
Apr 13　5:50 AM EST
May 12　4:47 PM EST

Jun 11　5:41 PM EST
Jul 10　8:48 PM EST
Aug 9　1:55 PM EST
Sep 8　8:15 AM EST
Oct 8　2:33 AM EST

Nov 6　7:36 PM EST
Dec 6 10:31 AM EST

• NIGHT LIGHT IN 2012 •

The boxes below depict **only** the nighttime portion of each day (night begins at the bottom of each box). The shaded bars indicate the relative amount of moonlight. The total length of each night is given in hours and miutes; times may vary by up to a few minutes by location (the times below are for Denver, Colorado).

Legend:
- Sunrise — NIGHT ENDS FOLLOWING DAY
- Sunset — NIGHT BEGINS
- Length of night
- No moon
- Moon above horizon with relative illumination

28

Day	JAN	FEB	MAR	APR	MAY	JUN	JUL	AUG	SEP	OCT	NOV	DEC
1	14h 35m	13h 49m	12h 40m	11h 19m	10h 5m	9h 12m	9h 4m	9h 47m	10h 58m	12h 15m	13h 32m	14h 26m
2	14h 34m	13h 47m	12h 37m	11h 16m	10h 3m	9h 11m	9h 5m	9h 49m	11h 1m	12h 18m	13h 34m	14h 28m
3	14h 34m	13h 45m	12h 34m	11h 13m	10h 1m	9h 9m	9h 6m	9h 51m	11h 3m	12h 20m	13h 37m	14h 29m
4	14h 33m	13h 43m	12h 32m	11h 11m	9h 59m	9h 9m	9h 7m	9h 53m	11h 6m	12h 23m	13h 39m	14h 30m
5	14h 32m	13h 40m	12h 29m	11h 8m	9h 57m	9h 8m	9h 7m	9h 56m	11h 8m	12h 25m	13h 41m	14h 31m
6	14h 31m	13h 38m	12h 27m	11h 6m	9h 54m	9h 7m	9h 8m	9h 57m	11h 11m	12h 28m	13h 43m	14h 32m
7	14h 30m	13h 36m	12h 24m	11h 3m	9h 52m	9h 6m	9h 9m	10h 0m	11h 13m	12h 31m	13h 45m	14h 33m
8	14h 29m	13h 34m	12h 21m	11h 1m	9h 51m	9h 5m	9h 10m	10h 2m	11h 16m	12h 33m	13h 47m	14h 34m
9	14h 28m	13h 31m	12h 19m	10h 58m	9h 49m	9h 5m	9h 11m	10h 4m	11h 19m	12h 36m	13h 49m	14h 34m
10	14h 27m	13h 29m	12h 16m	10h 56m	9h 46m	9h 4m	9h 12m	10h 6m	11h 21m	12h 38m	13h 51m	14h 35m
11	14h 25m	13h 27m	12h 14m	10h 53m	9h 44m	9h 3m	9h 13m	10h 8m	11h 24m	12h 41m	13h 53m	14h 36m
12	14h 24m	13h 24m	12h 11m	10h 51m	9h 42m	9h 3m	9h 14m	10h 10m	11h 26m	12h 43m	13h 55m	14h 36m
13	14h 23m	13h 22m	12h 8m	10h 48m	9h 40m	9h 2m	9h 16m	10h 13m	11h 29m	12h 46m	13h 57m	14h 37m
14	14h 21m	13h 20m	12h 6m	10h 46m	9h 39m	9h 2m	9h 17m	10h 15m	11h 31m	12h 48m	14h 0m	14h 38m
15	14h 20m	13h 17m	12h 3m	10h 43m	9h 37m	9h 1m	9h 18m	10h 17m	11h 34m	12h 51m	14h 1m	14h 38m
16	14h 18m	13h 15m	12h 0m	10h 41m	9h 35m	9h 1m	9h 20m	10h 20m	11h 36m	12h 53m	14h 3m	14h 38m
17	14h 17m	13h 12m	11h 58m	10h 37m	9h 33m	9h 1m	9h 21m	10h 22m	11h 39m	12h 55m	14h 5m	14h 38m
18	14h 15m	13h 10m	11h 55m	10h 36m	9h 31m	9h 1m	9h 23m	10h 24m	11h 42m	12h 58m	14h 7m	14h 38m
19	14h 14m	13h 7m	11h 53m	10h 33m	9h 30m	9h 1m	9h 24m	10h 27m	11h 44m	13h 1m	14h 9m	14h 41m
20	14h 12m	13h 5m	11h 50m	10h 31m	9h 28m	9h 1m	9h 26m	10h 29m	11h 47m	13h 3m	14h 10m	14h 39m
21	14h 10m	13h 2m	11h 47m	10h 28m	9h 26m	9h 1m	9h 28m	10h 31m	11h 49m	13h 6m	14h 12m	14h 39m
22	14h 9m	13h 0m	11h 45m	10h 26m	9h 25m	9h 1m	9h 29m	10h 34m	11h 52m	13h 8m	14h 14m	14h 39m
23	14h 7m	12h 58m	11h 42m	10h 24m	9h 23m	9h 1m	9h 31m	10h 36m	11h 55m	13h 11m	14h 15m	14h 38m
24	14h 5m	12h 55m	11h 39m	10h 21m	9h 22m	9h 2m	9h 32m	10h 38m	11h 57m	13h 13m	14h 17m	14h 38m
25	14h 3m	12h 53m	11h 37m	10h 19m	9h 20m	9h 2m	9h 34m	10h 41m	12h 0m	13h 15m	14h 18m	14h 38m
26	14h 1m	12h 50m	11h 34m	10h 17m	9h 19m	9h 2m	9h 36m	10h 44m	12h 2m	13h 18m	14h 20m	14h 38m
27	13h 59m	12h 47m	11h 32m	10h 14m	9h 18m	9h 3m	9h 38m	10h 46m	12h 5m	13h 20m	14h 21m	14h 37m
28	13h 57m	12h 45m	11h 29m	10h 12m	9h 17m	9h 3m	9h 39m	10h 48m	12h 7m	13h 23m	14h 23m	14h 37m
29	13h 55m	12h 42m	11h 26m	10h 10m	9h 15m	9h 3m	9h 41m	10h 51m	12h 10m	13h 25m	14h 24m	14h 37m
30	13h 53m		11h 24m	10h 7m	9h 14m	9h 4m	9h 43m	10h 54m	12h 13m	13h 27m	14h 25m	14h 36m
31	13h 51m		11h 21m		9h 13m		9h 45m	10h 56m		13h 30m		14h 35m

• HUNTING AND FISHING BY THE MOON •

Fishing

Most fishers are active when time and weather permit, factors that drive most outdoor hobbies. The lure of this sport has always included an element of luck, as fishing success—or the lack of it—often seems alienated from skill. And one highly visible factor—the Moon—has long played a key role in the quest to maximize luck. The rhythm of the tides, another observable phenomenon, has also been the source of fishing logic.

Research provides some evidence of these links, but does not always affirm what fishers would like to believe. In a mix of fresh- and saltwater experiments, studies have shown a pattern of increased feeding by some species during or close to full moons; other studies show different species with the opposite pattern, with the new moon of greater significance.

In large bodies of water, tides also suggest a correlation with fish activity, both mating and feeding, but typically with a lag between times of high or low tide and the peak of such activity.

If there is a consistant causal link between the Moon and fishing success, the most likely explanation is nighttime illumination. This

link could hold true for full and new moons as well as tides, as the monthly extremes of the latter are directly tied to the same two phases, although with a lag effect. See 2012 information about these natural cycles on pages 4–7, page 27, and page 28.

Hunting

Moonlight can be a boon for nighttime hunters, guiding them through unfamiliar terrain and helping them spot prey. It can also be a hindrance, because the same peak nighttime illumination generates a heightened sense of awareness in prey animals. Some wild animals are more active during the full moon; peak ac-

tivity for others falls during nights around the new moon, when there is no lunar illumination.

As with fishing, seasonal regulations, the availability of leisure time, and the weather are likely to play the largest role for hunters when it comes to finding time for this outdoor pursuit. But other than the two extremes for illumination from the Moon—full moon and new moon—the rising and setting times of all phases can provide a practical means for using nighttime hours, whether seeking or avoiding lunar light.

The chart on page 28 illustrates the prime times of every month for both cases: most and least nighttime illumination. The predicable rising and setting times of the Moon, coupled with the cycle of its phases, provide a guide for planning for either.

• GARDENING BY THE MOON •

Generations of gardeners attribute some or all of their green thumbs to traditional moon gardening lore. To improve gardening results, these guidelines assign specific gardening tasks to either the waxing or waning moon cycles (the "light of the moon" and the "dark of the moon"). The most articulated of these guidelines segregate activities according to the quarter phase, something not indicated here. Some gardening traditions also add in the movement of the Moon through the twelve astrological signs as a point of reference, based on their four basic attributes—earth, air, water, and fire—and two general aspects—barren and fruitful.

2012 WAXING
Light of the Moon

January 1	January 9
January 23	February 7
February 21	March 8
March 22	April 6
April 21	May 6
May 20	June 4
June 19	July 3
July 19	August 2
August 17	August 31
September 16	September 30
October 15	October 29
November 13	November 28
December 13	December 28

2012 WANING
Dark of the Moon

January 9	January 23
February 7	February 21
March 8	March 22
April 6	April 21
May 6	May 20
June 4	June 19
July 3	July 19
August 2	August 17
August 31	September 16
September 30	October 15
October 29	November 13
November 28	December 13
December 28	January 11, 2013

• 2012 MOON WAXING •

Plant for leaf	TAU	CAN	SCO	PIS	
Plant for grain	GEM	CAN	LIB	SCO	
Plant for vine	ARI	GEM	CAN	SCO	AQU
Plant for fruit	GEM	CAN	LIB	SCO	
Plant for winter	ARI	TAU	GEM	CAN	CAP
Harvest	ARI	VIR	SCO	SAG	PIS
Harvest leaf	ARI	CAN	SCO	PIS	
Harvest fruit	ARI	LEO	SAG	AQU	
Fertilize (quick acting)	ARI	CAN	SCO	CAP	PIS
Prune to set	ARI	GEM	SCO	SAG	AQU
Prune to limit	ARI	LEO	SAG		
Control pests	LEO	VIR	CAP		
Irrigate	CAN	LIB	SCO	PIS	
Cultivate	ARI	TAU	SAG	AQU	PIS

• 2012 MOON WANING •

Plant for root	TAU	CAN	SCO	CAP	PIS	
Plant for seed	GEM	CAN	SCO	PIS		
Plant for trees	ARI	CAN	SCO	SAG	CAP	PIS
Harvest for storage	ARI	GEM	LEO	SAG	AQU	
Harvest for canning	TAU	CAN	LEO	SCO	PIS	
Harvest for drying	ARI	LEO	SAG	AQU		
Fertilize (slow acting)	TAU	CAN	SAG	CAP	PIS	
Prune to lessen	ARI	LEO	SAG			
Compost	CAN	VIR	SCO	PIS		
Irrigate	TAU	CAN	SCO	PIS		
Cultivate	ARI	LEO	SAG			

• MOON SIGNS IN 2012 •

One of the oldest traditions in almanacs is the application of astrology, especially the movements of the moon through the twelve signs of the zodiac. The chart below is based on Universal Time (UT). See page 2 to correct for local time zones in the United States.

	1	2	3	4	5	6	7	8	9	10	11	12	13	14	15	16	17	18	19	20	21	22	23	24	25	26	27	28	29	30	31
JAN	ARI	TAU 22:15	TAU	TAU	GEM 10:44	GEM	CAN 21:05	CAN	CAN	LEO 04:35	LEO	VIR 09:44	VIR	LIB 13:28	LIB	SCO 16:33	SCO	SAG 19:28	SAG	CAP 22:40	CAP ●	CAP	AQU 21:52	AQU	PIS 09:11	PIS	ARI 18:27	ARI	ARI	TAU 06:28	TAU
FEB	GEM 19:14	GEM	GEM	CAN 06:03	CAN	LEO 13:23	LEO	VIR 17:32	VIR	LIB 19:54	LIB	SCO 22:01	SCO	SCO	SAG 00:56	SAG	CAP 05:03	CAP	AQU 10:28	AQU	PIS 17:31 ●	PIS	PIS	ARI 02:47	ARI	TAU 14:29	TAU	TAU	GEM 03:26		
MAR	GEM	CAN 15:08	CAN	LEO 23:17	LEO	LEO	VIR 03:26	VIR	LIB 04:50	LIB	SCO 05:23	SCO	SAG 06:53	SAG	CAP 10:23	CAP	AQU 16:11	AQU	AQU	PIS 00:05	PIS	ARI 09:57 ●	ARI	TAU 21:43	TAU	TAU	GEM 11:43	GEM	GEM	CAN 00:07	CAN
APR	LEO 09:35	LEO	VIR 14:52	VIR	LIB 16:32	LIB	SCO 16:17	SCO	SAG 16:12	SAG	CAP 18:01	CAP	AQU 22:47	AQU	AQU	PIS 06:37	PIS	ARI 16:58	ARI	ARI	TAU 05:05 ●	TAU	GEM 18:05	GEM	GEM	CAN 06:42	CAN	LEO 17:10	LEO	LEO	
MAY	VIR 00:02	VIR	LIB 03:03	LIB	SCO 03:19	SCO	SAG 02:38	SAG	CAP 02:59	CAP	AQU 06:02	AQU	PIS 12:41	PIS	ARI 22:45	ARI	ARI	TAU 11:03	TAU	TAU ●	GEM 00:05	GEM	CAN 12:31	CAN	LEO 23:11	LEO	LEO	VIR 07:06	VIR	LIB 11:45	LIB
JUN	SCO 13:31	SCO	SAG 13:32	SAG	CAP 13:30	CAP	AQU 15:16	AQU	PIS 20:21	PIS	PIS	ARI 05:21	ARI	TAU 17:21	TAU	TAU	GEM 06:23	GEM	CAN 18:33 ●	CAN	CAN	LEO 04:47	LEO	VIR 12:42	VIR	LIB 18:15	LIB	SCO 21:32	SCO	SAG 23:03	
JUL	SAG	CAP 23:50	CAP	CAP	AQU 01:25	AQU	PIS 05:29	PIS	ARI 13:13	ARI	ARI	TAU 00:30	TAU	GEM 13:26	GEM	GEM	CAN 01:31	CAN	LEO 11:13 ●	LEO	VIR 18:24	VIR	LIB 23:38	LIB	LIB	SCO 03:29	SCO	SAG 06:17	SAG	CAP 08:29	CAP
AUG	AQU 10:55	AQU	PIS 14:57	PIS	ARI 21:58	ARI	ARI	TAU 08:27	TAU	GEM 21:10	GEM	GEM	CAN 09:27	CAN	LEO 19:04	LEO	LEO ●	VIR 01:33	VIR	LIB 05:45	LIB	SCO 08:53	SCO	SAG 11:50	SAG	CAP 14:58	CAP	AQU 18:38	AQU	PIS 23:30	PIS
SEP	PIS	ARI 06:37	ARI	TAU 16:41	TAU	TAU	GEM 05:09	GEM	CAN 17:49	CAN	CAN	LEO 04:00	LEO	VIR 10:30	VIR	LIB 13:55 ●	LIB	SCO 15:45	SCO	SAG 17:33	SAG	CAP 20:20	CAP	CAP	AQU 00:32	AQU	PIS 06:23	PIS	ARI 14:13	ARI	
OCT	ARI	TAU 00:26	TAU	GEM 12:46	GEM	GEM	CAN 01:45	CAN	LEO 12:54	LEO	VIR 20:23	VIR	VIR	LIB 00:01	LIB ●	SCO 01:06	SCO	SAG 01:25	SAG	CAP 02:40	CAP	CAP	AQU 06:02	AQU	PIS 11:59	PIS	ARI 20:30	ARI	ARI	TAU 06:15	GEM 18:40
NOV	GEM	GEM	CAN 07:43	CAN	LEO 19:39	LEO	LEO	VIR 04:34	VIR	LIB 09:34	LIB	SCO 11:10	SCO ●	SAG 10:51	SAG	CAP 10:35	CAP	AQU 12:10	AQU	PIS 16:54	PIS	PIS	ARI 01:11	ARI	TAU 12:18	TAU	TAU	GEM 00:58	GEM	CAN 13:54	
DEC	CAN	CAN	LEO 01:56	LEO	VIR 11:51	VIR	LIB 18:35	LIB	SCO 21:50	SCO	SCO	SAG 22:21	SAG ●	SAG	AQU 21:52	AQU	AQU	PIS 00:48	PIS	ARI 07:43	ARI	TAU 18:25	TAU	TAU	GEM 07:13	GEM	CAN 20:06	CAN	LEO 07:45	LEO	LEO

ARI Aries   **TAU** Taurus   **GEM** Gemini   **CAN** Cancer   **LEO** Leo   **VIR** Virgo   **SCO** Scorpio   **LIB** Libra   **SAG** Sagittarius   **CAP** Capricorn   **AQU** Aquarius   **PIS** Pisces

Moon Resources

THE MOON ALMANAC www.themoonalmanac.com
THE MOON CALENDAR www.themooncalendar.com

SKY SIGHTS

- **This Week's Sky at a Glance (Sky & Telescope)**
  www.skyandtelescope.com
- **North American Skies**
  home.comcast.net/~sternmann/Welcome.html
- **EarthSky Tonight**
  www.earthsky.org

MOON ASTRONOMY

- **U.S. Naval Observatory**
  www.usno.navy.mil/astronomy
- **USGS Astrogeology Science Center**
  http://astrogeology.usgs.gov/SolarSystem/Earth/Moon

WHAT THE MOON LOOKS LIKE

- http://aa.usno.navy.mil/idltemp/current_moon.php

MOON CALCULATORS & CYCLE DATA

- http://aa.usno.navy.mil/faq/docs/moon_phases
- http://aa.usno.navy.mil/data/docs/RS_OneYear.php
- http://moon-phase-calculator.software.informer.com

TIDE PREDICTIONS

- **Tides & Currents (NOAA)**
  http://co-ops.nos.noaa.gov

ECLIPSE INFORMATION

- http://aa.usno.navy.mil/data/docs/UpcomingEclipses.php

CRESCENT MOON VISIBILITY

- http://aa.usno.navy.mil/faq/docs/islamic.php
- www.jgiesen.de/nmo/index.html

PLANETARIUM & SKY SOFTWARE

- **Stellarium**
  www.stellarium.org
- **Quick Phase Calculator**
  www.calculatorcat.com/moon_phases
- **Lunar Map Pro**
  www.riti.com/prodserv_lunarmappro.htm
- **SkyX/Software Bisque**
  www.bisque.com

ORGANIZATIONS

- **American Association of Amateur Astronomers**
  www.astromax.com
- **American Astronomical Society**
  www.aas.org
- **Astronomical League**
  www.astroleague.org
- **National Space Science Data Center (NASA)**
  www.nssdc.gsfc.nasa.gov

- **Astronomical Society of the Pacific**
  www.astrosociety.org
- **British Astronomical Association**
  www.britastro.org
- **Royal Astronomical Society of Canada**
  www.rasc.ca
- **International Occultation and Timing Association**
  www.lunar-occultations.com
- **The International Planetarian Society**
  www.ips-planetarium.org

MAGAZINES

- *Amateur Astronomy Magazine*
  www.amateurastronomy.com
- *Astronomy Magazine*
  www.astronomy.com
- *Nature Magazine*
  www.nature.com
- *The Old Farmer's Almanac*
  www.almanac.com
- *Popular Astronomy Magazine*
  www.popastro.com
- *Sky & Telescope Magazine*
  www.skyandtelescope.com
- *Sky News*
  www.skynews.ca